Titus Maccius Plautus
The Captives

Translation by David Bolton

Published by Lulu Books

2019

Copyright by David Bolton

ISBN 978-0-244-82409-9

Terms for the performance of this play may be obtained from
David Bolton at dgbolton0@gmail.com.

All translations in this edition, including the introductory sections (unless
specifically attributed) are by David Bolton.

Colour: #C3161C

3

Contents

Titus Maccius Plautus

References in the works of Cicero suggest that Plautus was born c254 BC and died c184 BC. Festus (2nd century AD) says he was born in Sarsina in Umbria in Northern Italy.

Few details of his life are known. There is even doubt about his name: Maccius Plautus could be interpreted as 'Clown Flatfoot'. As to his life, some evidence comes from Aulus Gellius, who, referring to the works of Varro, says "Varro and many others have recorded that he wrote *Saturio*, *Addictus* and a third comedy, the name of which now escapes me, whilst working in a bakery, since, having lost in trade all the money he earned whilst employed in the theatre, he returned destitute to Rome and, to earn a livelihood, he found a job with a baker turning a mill, called a 'hand-mill'."[1] His 'employment in the theatre' presumably would include general work as a stagehand and constructing scenery. His later work in the bakery would have been low-paid, and would have involved operating a mill with two handles, requiring two men to push or turn them. The strength of Gellius' evidence is disputed: it is suggested that the story may have attached itself to Plautus since characters in his plays are often threatened with 'working the mill'. Conversely, of course, this threat could appear frequently in Plautus because of his own personal experience.

Ancient Sarsina was situated in a rural area of North Eastern Italy and Plautus was perhaps unlikely to become acquainted there with either the theatre or, more especially, the Greek theatre. Gellius says of him that 'he returned … to Rome' after his failed commercial venture.

---

[1] Aulus Gellius, *Noctes Atticae* III. 3

How Plautus developed his Latin style, learnt Greek and studied Greek literature is unknown. Perhaps, he left Sarsina for Rome, got caught up in the theatre, and developed the necessary skills in the process.

The twenty-one extant comedies (some being fragmentary) are considered to have been written in the last twenty or twenty-five years of his life, that is, after, say, 209 BC until his death in 184 BC, that is, from around age 45 or 50 to his death at the age of about 70 [1].

The dates of the first performances of most plays, however, are uncertain. *Saturio, Addictus* and the third comedy referred to by Gellius appear to have been early works. Gellius adds: "There are about one hundred and thirty comedies ascribed to Plautus, but L. Aelius, a most learned man, judged only twenty-five to be his. But there is no doubt that those that do not seem to have been written by Plautus whilst attributed with his name, were by ancient playwrights, and were reworked and polished by him. Consequently they smack of the Plautine style"[2].

---

[1] Discussed by G. E. Duckworth, *Nature of Roman Comedy: a Study in Popular Entertainment*

[2] Aulus Gellius, *Noctes Atticae* III. 3

Roman comedy

The Greek Old Comedy, performed at the Athenian Dionysia and represented by Aristophanes is associated with the fifth century BC. Little is known of later comedy production until the late fourth century, when Greek New Comedy emerged. The choruses of the earlier Greek plays fell away and dramas took more the format of modern plays. Stock characters emerged: young men in love, slaves cleverer than their masters, female slaves who turn out to be well-born, braggart soldiers, irascible old men who complain about their wives, hungry parasites and greedy slave dealers.

The writers of these comedies include Menander, Philemon and Diphilus of the late fourth and early third centuries. Roman playwrights such as Plautus and Terence took the original plays of these playwrights and did not simply translate them but rewrote them. As Plautus says of the play *Casina*, in its Prologue, "In Greek, the play is called *Clerumenoe*, which means 'The drawing of lots'. Diphilus wrote the play in Greek, and later, Plautus, starting afresh, in Latin". Plautus is known to have reworked the plays of Menander, Philemon, Diphilus and also the minor playwright Demophilus.

Whilst the action of each play takes place in some Greek city (eg. Athens, Sicyon, Epidamnus or Epidaurus), and the actors wore Greek clothes, the references remain Roman: Roman gods, the Roman forum, Rome's magistrates, laws and law courts, the Roman Senate and places in and around Rome.

The Greek clothes of the actors would in particular have included the *pallium* or cloak for the (non-slave) male characters (hence this form of play or *fabula* was called *'palliata'*). Male characters generally wore tunics as the basic item of clothing. There is some debate as to whether masks were worn; being comedy, there would no doubt be some elements of outlandish appearance.

At least part of each play was given musical accompaniment: the surviving texts of the six plays of Terence state that one Flaccus Claudi performed at each first performance of each play on a variety of reed flutes. Commentators have examined the metrical structure of the plays. There is some consensus that some of the dialogue was spoken, but that much of the dialogue and speeches were 'sung', that is, either chanted or sung as recitative to the accompaniment of the flute. There do not appear, however, to have been 'arias' or songs as such.

The plays were performed during Games held as part of religious festivals. The plays of Terence give details of the Games at which his plays were first performed. These include the *Ludi Megalenses* in honour of the Goddess Cybele also known as *Magna Mater*, the *Ludi Romani* in honour of Jupiter, and the Funeral Games held for L. Aemilius Paulus. In other words, they were held at each of the annual *Ludi* and at other one-off important occasions such as a public funeral.

The actors will often have been slaves, who may have been beaten if their performance was poor. They certainly asked for applause at the end of each play. The Epilogue to Plautus' *Cistellaria* (*The Casket*) sums this up:

"Audience, don't expect the actors to appear on stage again: that's the end of the play! They're taking their costumes off now, and the actor who forgot his lines will be given a beating, and the one who didn't will get a drink.

All that remains, is for you, in time honoured fashion, to give us a round of applause."

Roman theatres developed from wooden structures to elaborate stone ones. For the actors, there appear to have been entrances from the wings, a central entrance, and further entrances on either side of the central entrance. This arrangement conveniently fits the set of most Roman comedies, which often present two houses with a street running in front of or between them.

The plays had to appeal to a broad audience. They were studied by literary men such as Varro and Cicero, but they also had to appeal to the Roman populace at large, many of whom would have little or no literary interest, and many of the foreigners in Rome would have little Latin. They also had competition from rival, non-literary performances: Terence tells of the problems he once encountered: "As soon as I began to show it [my play], the challenges of boxers (also the expectation of some tight-rope dancers), the crowds of followers, the noise and the shouts of women, made me finish with the play before the conclusion. I began to apply my old methods to this new play as a trial. I presented it afresh. The first act was well received. Meanwhile, a rumour circulated that a gladiatorial contest was to be held: the crowds gathered; they jostled and shouted and fought for their place."[1]

Yet the Latin of Plautus and Terence is well crafted (though idiomatic) and often in complex verse form. Perhaps, then, it is possible to underestimate the Roman audiences, who must in fact have appreciated the literary aspects of the plays.

[1] Terence, *Hecyra*, Prologus (II)

The broad appeal required of his plays may have led Plautus in particular to be influenced by two earlier Italian theatrical traditions: the Atellane plays and the form of play developed by Livius Andronicus. Livy says that in the mid-fourth century 'scenic games' were introduced; the actors were from Etruria and there were no words but only dancing to the flute; these were imitated locally with the introduction of comic verses and actions to suit the words; this became an accepted form; but then, Livius Andronicus first produced a play with a plot; his plays had spoken dialogue, but also large sections delivered with words 'sung' or chanted to flutes; whilst such plays were left to actors, young men again performed comic verses, known as '*exodia*', or 'after-verses', which were strung together to form 'Atellane plays'; these were of Oscan origin.[1]

St Jerome read Plautus at the end of the fourth century AD; but Plautus received little interest in the Middle Ages, unlike Terence who continued to be copied and read. Plautus resurfaced, however, and influenced Shakespeare, whose *Comedy of Errors* reflects *Menaechmi*, Ben Jonson, whose *The Case is Altered* reflects *Aulularia* and *Captivi*, Molière, whose *L'Avare* is based on *Aulularia*, and many others including Stephen Sondheim's *A Funny Thing Happened on the Way to the Forum* (*Pseudolus*, *Miles Gloriosus* and *Mostellaria*).

---

[1] Livy, *History of Rome* VII. 2

The Captives (Captivi)

The plays of Plautus are generally thought to be reworkings of earlier plays of the Greek New Comedy. Yet it is not known what, if any, such play *The Captives* is based on. Whilst it was probably written in the last twenty-five years of Plautus' life, it is not known when it was first produced.

The play contains some elements that are well known to Roman comedy: a prologue sets the scene so that the action can commence with the audience fully apprised of the circumstances surrounding the main characters; and the parasite, Ergasilus, is a stock character who provides light-hearted humour as he vainly tries to win dinner invitations.

Prologues often say how the play will end, eg, that a slave girl will prove to be a free-born citizen, and that she will therefore be able to marry her admirer. This prologue, however, gives a vital piece of information unknown to the characters on stage, viz. that the captive, Tyndarus, is in fact the son of his captor, Hegio. Without this piece of information, much of the irony in the dialogue would be lost upon the audience.

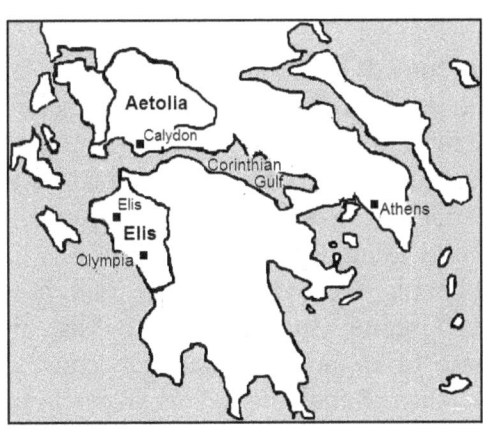

The play is set in Aetolia, a Greek state, but no particular Aetolian city is mentioned as the home of Hegio. The war between Aetolia and Elis, referred to in the play, is fictional. Aetolia, in particular, may have been well known in Rome because of its control during this period of the Aetolian League: a sphere of influence in Central and Northern Greece against Macedon to the north. However, Plautus could have chosen any Greek state as the setting for his play. The set of *The Captives*, as was common in Roman comedies, featured two houses with a street running in front of or between them.

Two of the characters, Tyndarus and Philocrates, are genuinely noble in their actions. Tyndarus, as a well-treated slave of Philocrates takes considerable risks in conspiring to have is master escape from his captivity. Philocrates, for his part, honours his bargain with Hegio in that he secures the release of Hegio's son and takes the risk of returning with him to his former captor in order to ensure the son's safe return and to recover his slave whom he left behind.

Hegio, the father who has had both his sons taken from him, has a carefully drawn multi-faceted character. He shows distaste for the business of buying prisoners, a certain naïvity in being hoodwinked by them, distraction when he feels he has lost his sons altogether, a hasty temper and vindictiveness in his treatment of Tyndarus, and finally, a certain sympathy.

The action of a Roman comedy is assumed to be (more or less) continuous. Rather as in a Greek tragedy, the action generally takes place within a single day. In this play there are anomalies in the passage of time. Ergasilus speaks as if the action were from a morning to late afternoon: In Act 3.1, he declares his intention of going to the port; in Act 4.1, he returns from the port having seen Hegio's son. But it is obvious that Philocrates' journey from Aetolia to Elis, his negotiation of the release of Hegio's son and his return to Aetolia (picking up the slave Stalagmus on the way) must have taken weeks rather than days. Also, Tyndarus, put to forced labour in the quarries, has clearly undergone weeks rather than an hour or so of exhausting work. A modern production must therefore make it clear that several weeks have elapsed between the actions of Acts 3 and 4, and allow for the impression that Ergasilus is talking about a morning and an afternoon several weeks apart.

The capture of the slave Stalagmus (who stole the boy known to us now as Tyndarus) is necessary for the identification of Tyndarus as Hegio's son. Plautus, however, in his eagerness to maintain the pace of his tale and to bring his play to a conclusion, gives no explanation as to where or how the elusive Stalagmus was recognized and apprehended. The audience is simply asked to believe in a chance encounter.

Roman comedies often had characters with comic names, and here, 'Stalagmus', the name of the thieving slave, means in Greek a 'dripping (of liquid)' and was occasionally used derisively of a man of small stature. Other names are of significance: 'Philocrates' suggests power, 'Philopolemus' suggests a 'lover of war', perhaps ironically since he was a prisoner of war, and 'Hegio' perhaps suggests leadership.

A typical Roman comedy has as its theme a young man (or perhaps an old man) falling in love with a beautiful but apparently wholly inappropriate young woman; this gives rise to much bawdy humour before the matter is resolved. *The Captives*, however, had a theme that was thought-provoking and relevant to a nation regularly at war: the need for humanity in the treatment of prisoners of war. Hegio, who has absolute power over the prisoners he holds, is asked how he would like is own son, held as a prisoner of war, to be treated. The irony, made known to the audience in the Prologue, is that one of Hegio's prisoners *is* his own son: and that this is the prisoner whom Hegio treats with great vindictiveness.

There is a curious parallel between *The Captives* and the story of M Atilius Regulus, a Roman general who participated in the defeat of the Carthaginians in a sea-battle off Sicily in the First Punic War (mid-3rd century BC). He defeated the Carthaginians again in North Africa, but was eventually captured by them. He is said to have persuaded them to let him return to Rome to negotiate a peace or at least a return of prisoners, on condition that he would then return to Carthage. Once in Rome, however, he is said to have encouraged the Romans to prosecute the war against Carthage with renewed vigour, and then to have honoured his pledge by returning to Carthage, where he was tortured to death. There is considerable doubt about the truth of the story of his journey to Rome and return to Carthage: it may well be a legend – of which our earliest record dates from the late 2nd century BC.

The Captives

(The Plot and the Dramatis Personae set out on pages 19 and 21 derive from the transmitted editions of the play.)

The Plot

Captured in battle was Hegio's son;
A slave had stolen and sold a second son;
Prepared to make exchange for his captured son,
The father buys Elean prisoners,
Including, unbeknown, the stolen son.
Vestments exchanged, this son's own master gained
Escape, returning with the captured son.
Sons true were both then recognized to be.

[1] The Plot is thought not to have been written by Plautus.

Dramatis Personae[1]

Ergasilus, a parasite

Hegio, an old man

Overseer

Philocrates, a young man

Tyndarus, a slave

Aristophontes, a young man

Boy

Philpolemus, a young man

Stalagmus, a slave

---

[1] The Prologue is delivered by a member of the cast; Ergasilus, a parasite and scrounger; Hegio, an old man of Aetolia; Overseer, a slave of Hegio; Philocrates, a captive, a young man from Elis; Tyndarus, a slave of Philocrates, also captive; Aristophontes, a captive, a young man from Elis; Boy, a young slave of Hegio; Philopolemus, Hegio's son; Stalagmus, a slave of Hegio; There is also Colax together with other (non-speaking) servants of Hegio.

21

The Captives

Scene: Aetolia; the houses of Hegio and Hegio's brother face on to the street.

Tyndarus, *dressed as a slave, and* Philocrates, *wearing a good quality tunic, are standing in chains outside Hegio's house.*

PROLOGUE

You see those two prisoners standing there? What can I say about them? Well, they're standing not sitting! You are my witnesses I'm telling the truth.

Now then, the old man who lives here (*indicating Hegio's house*) is the father of this one here (*indicating Tyndarus*).

And how *he* came to be a slave of his own father, I'm going to explain, if you wouldn't mind paying attention.

The old man in fact had two sons. But a slave stole one of them – this one here – when he was a four year old, and ran off with him and sold him in Elis to the father of this one here (*indicating Philocrates*).

Now, have you got that? I hope so. How about you at the back, sir? I'm not going to rupture myself getting you lot to understand all this. But if you've taken it in so far, I'll give you a bit more of the story.

The slave I was talking about fled his master, took the little boy (*indicating Tyndarus*) with him and sold the boy to this man's (*indicating Philocrates*) father. He, after he'd bought the boy, took him and gave him to his son, as his very own, since he was about the same age.

Now, this boy (*indicating Tyndarus*) is home again – a slave of his own father. But his father has no idea who he really is. Yes, the gods kick us about like footballs!
And now you know how the old man lost one of his sons.

Later on, when Aetolia was at war with Elis, as often happens in war, the other son was captured. And he was bought by a doctor, called Menarchus, who lived in that same part of Elis.
The old man, here, started to buy Elean prisoners of war, to see if he could find one that he could exchange for the son of his who had been captured. He did not realise he had bought his other son. And yesterday, he heard that an Elean cavalry officer of the highest rank and family had been taken prisoner. He would spare no expense to save his son. And so, with a view to getting his son home, he bought both of these two from the officers who were selling them.

However.... These two have agreed a plan between themselves to enable the slave (*indicating Tyndarus*) to get his master (*indicating Philocrates*) back home again. Accordingly, they are going to swap clothes and names. Tyndarus here is to call himself Philocrates; and Philocrates here is to call himself Tyndarus. They are going to pretend to be one another. And Tyndarus here, in the guise of Philocrates will put his plan skilfully into action and help to secure his master's freedom.
He will also, as it will turn out, rescue his brother – the other stolen son – and bring him home, a free man, to his father – without at first realizing it. As so often happens, a man can do more good by chance than he does by design.

Anyway, without fully understanding the true situation, they have put their heads together, concocted their stories and planned their trickery – all with the effect that this Tyndarus might remain in servitude here in his father's house. In his ignorance, he is a slave of his own father. We poor men, what hope do we have, when I come to think of it?

This will be the action of our play. It will just be a story to you. But I'd like to give a few words of advice. It will be much to your advantage to pay attention to our play. This isn't your standard comedy. There's no unrepeatable bad language. There's no perjured slave dealer, or evil courtesan, or braggart soldier. And have no fear because I mentioned that the Aetolians are at war with the Eleans. All the battles are well off-stage. It would be quite an injustice if we, in our comic costumes, had suddenly to present a tragedy. So if anyone's looking for a fight.... not in here please!

And so farewell. Be good judges of our excellent tale!

(*Exit* Prologue; *Enter* Overseer *from Hegio's house, who takes charge of Tydarus and Philocrates. Then exeunt* Overseer, Tyndarus *and* Philocrates *into Hegio's house.*)

ACT 1

(Enter Ergasilus *from along the street.)*

ERGASILUS My name is Ergasilus, but young men around
here all call me Imagain! Yes, Imagain. And why's
that then? Well, it's because when I turn up at one of
their dinners they all shout out "Oh no, not Imagain".
If I'm invited to dinner, I turn up; and if I'm not
invited, well, I've a right to eat as much as the next
man, and so I turn up anyway. I'm not put off by the
'delicacies' of the situation; no, I eat anything! We
scroungers are like mice: we can always eat our way
through other people's food!
When the holiday times come, when men disappear
into the country, then it is a holiday time for our
stomachs. We are like little snails hiding in their
shells in hot weather, when there's no dew for them
to suck. We scroungers are the same: in the holidays
we have to hide miserably in our shells whilst the
people we sponge off, go off and holiday their
holidays away. In other ways, we behave like dogs.
During the holidays, we are lean hunters; but when
the holidays are over, we are the wolves, fierce, all-
devouring!
If a scrounger doesn't like the treatment he receives,
if he gets fed up of being a punchbag and having pots
cracked over his head, he can always pack his bags,
go through the Triple Gate[1] and try his luck in the
next town.

---

[1] The Porta Trigemina was a gate of Ancient Rome at the foot
of the Aventine Hill.

There's a danger I might have to do exactly that. My patron has been captured by our enemies. Aetolia is at war with Elis; and this is Aetolia and he's a prisoner in Elis. He's called Philopolemus and he's the son of old man Hegio who lives here. What a sad house this is: every time I look at it, I want to cry! Now this Hegio, for the sake of his son, has begun to ply a trade which is distasteful to him and quite out of character. He is buying up enemy prisoners to see if he can find one he can exchange for his son. And I hope he succeeds, because if he doesn't get him back, I see no way of getting back my former life! I can't place any hope in the young men of today: they all love themselves too much! He, however, is a young man of the old school. I have never helped smooth his wrinkled brow without receiving some benefit in return. The father is worthy of the son: and I'm going to see him now.

(*The door of Hegio's house begins to open.*)
But his door is opening.
How often have I come out through that door well fed and watered!

[1.2]
(*Enter* Hegio *and* Overseer *from Hegio's house.*)

HEGIO Pay attention now. Those two prisoners… I bought them yesterday from the officers… put them in single chains… take off the heavier ones that are on them now. Let them walk about if they want to – inside or out – but make sure they are well guarded. A free captive is like a wild bird – it doesn't take much for them to escape, and then you can never get hold of them again.

27

OVERSEER Well, I suppose we'd all rather be free than slaves.

HEGIO You haven't made much effort to buy your freedom.

OVERSEER I haven't anything to give you – other than a clean pair of heels!

HEGIO I wouldn't try that; or I'll have something to give you.

OVERSEER Perhaps I could become that wild bird you mentioned.

HEGIO You'd soon find yourself in a cage all day.
Anyway, that's enough of that. Remember my orders; go look to the prisoners. I'm going round to my brother's to inspect my other prisoners and to make sure they didn't cause any trouble last night. Then I'll be coming home again.

(*Exit* Overseer *into Hegio's house.*)

ERGASILUS (*to audience*) I feel sorry for that poor old man, having to engage in the wretched incarceration business for the sake of his son. Mind you, if it helps him get his son back, he can enter the public execution business for all I care.

HEGIO Who's that over there?

ERGASILUS (*Weeping histrionically*) It is I, a man who feels your pain, wastes away, grows old and languishes as wretchedly as you do. I'm so thin, I'm just skin and bone. Nothing I eat seems to do me any good – (*aside*) at home, that is: I find dining out is much more to my taste!

HEGIO Ergasilus! Good day.

ERGASILUS (*continues weeping*) May the Gods be with you, Hegio.

HEGIO Don't cry.

ERGASILUS Not cry for your son? Not cry for such a young man as he?

HEGIO I always felt you were a good friend of my son, and he of you.

ERGASILUS We mortals only realise the extent of our blessings when we lose them. And I, only after your son fell into the hands of the enemy, did I realise how much he means to me.

HEGIO If you, unconnected to him, bear his loss so ill, how do you think I feel to lose the only son I have?

ERGASILUS Unconnected to him?! Ah Hegio, don't ever say that. Don't ever think such a thing! He may the only son you have; but he is the only one more than 'only' to me.

HEGIO I find it commendable that the disaster that has befallen my son you take so much on your own shoulders; but do try to cheer up.

ERGASILUS What really grieves me is that the whole Catering Corps is lost.

HEGIO But couldn't you find someone for the time being to command another Catering Corps?

ERGASILUS No one wants the job since Philopolemus was captured.

HEGIO I'm not surprised. You expect cohorts of bakers and confectioners, legions of gamekeepers and butchers and fruit-growers, not to mention a whole navy to keep you in seafood!

ERGASILUS (*aside*) How often lights are kept under bushels! This man should be made a general forthwith!

HEGIO Anyway, cheer up! I'm sure we'll get him home in a matter of days, because in here (*indicating his house*), I have a young prisoner from one of the highest and wealthiest families of Elis. I've every expectation of exchanging him for my son.

ERGASILUS May all the Gods and Goddesses help you.

By the way, you haven't been invited out to dinner somewhere, have you?

HEGIO Not so far as I know. Why do you ask?

ERGASILUS It's just that it's my birthday today; and I'd like to invite you to your house to dinner.

HEGIO How generous! You'd have to be satisfied with a small portion.

ERGASILUS Not too small a portion, please. That's what I have every day at home.

Right then! Let's strike a bargain,...provided I don't get a better offer of course..., I'll say the pleasure of my company has been "Sold to you, Sir!"...my terms and conditions apply, of course, and I'm as careful about the terms and conditions as if I were selling a gold mine.

HEGIO More of a bottomless pit, in your case!

If you must, perhaps you could come round some other time?

ERGASILUS But I'm free now!

HEGIO The road to my dinner table is long and hard. And whilst you're aiming at a juicy steak, so far you barely warrant a bowl of gruel!

ERGASILUS You won't get rid of me that easily, Hegio. I shall come round with my teeth sharpened and polished!

HEGIO But my meat has gone off.

ERGASILUS Then bring it back!

HEGIO My food is plain.

ERGASILUS I'm sure it's solid!

HEGIO Mainly earthy vegetables.

ERGASILUS We're not aiming at the stars.

Now is there anything I can do for you?
HEGIO Come round ...*later*.
ERGASILUS I'll be there!

(*Exit* Ergasilus *along the street.*)

HEGIO I have to go in now... and do some reckoning up to see how much I have deposited with my bankers. Then I'm off to my brother's, as I said before.

(*Exit* Hegio *into his house.*)

ACT 2

(*Enter* Overseer, Tyndarus *and* Philocrates *from Hegio's house. Tyndarus and Philocrates are wearing lighter chains and have swapped clothes.*)

OVERSEER If the immortal gods have willed it that you undergo such hardship, you had best endure it with equanimity. Doing so will make your captivity easier to bear. You were free men at home, I believe, but when slavery comes along, it's a good policy to humour it and your master's authority, and so make it as easy as possible for yourselves. Your master's actions are deemed to be proper, even if they are not.

PHILOCRATES ⎱ (*wailing*) Oh oh oh.
TYNDARUS ⎰

OVERSEER There's no point in wailing or tearful eyes. It helps to be positive in difficult circumstances.

TYNDARUS But we find it shameful to be in chains.

OVERSEER Our master would find it more regrettable if, having paid good money for you, he removed your chains and allowed you to go free.

TYNDARUS What does he have to fear from us? We know what our duty would be if he allowed us to go free.

OVERSEER You're planning to escape. I know what you're up to!

PHILOCRATES Us, escape? Where would we escape to?

OVERSEER You'd go back home.

PHILOCRATES What! That wouldn't be right – to behave like runaway slaves!

OVERSEERS By the Gods, if the chance arose, why not take it?!

TYNDARUS Would you please grant us one request?

OVERSEER Which is?

32

TYNDARUS Allow us two to speak together in private.

OVERSEER All right, I'll stand over here. (*He moves further down the street.*) But don't talk for too long!

TYNDARUS I won't, and we are indebted to you.

PHILOCRATES (*to Tyndarus*) Come over here now (*moving further away from Overseer*). We don't want our words overheard and our plans laid bare. Schemes are not schemes unless they are carefully looked after; and if they become known, they will be a source of... (*indicating of his back*) ...great pain.

Now, if you are to be my master and I pretend to be your slave, we need considerable care and caution so that our plan can be hatched coolly, precisely and with great attention to detail, without being spotted. We have a big test ahead of us; we need to keep our eyes open.

TYNDARUS You want me to play the part of being your former master?

PHILOCRATES Yes indeed.

TYNDARUS You now see that for the sake of your own dear self, I am holding my own dear neck cheap.

PHILOCRATES I know that.

TYNDARUS I hope you remember it when you have achieved your aim. Men, for the most part, have the habit of being your best friend when they want a favour doing, but when they have what they want, they suddenly change and will be as deceitful as you like. I'd like to make clear what I expect of you.

PHILOCRATES But you are like a second father to me!

TYNDARUS Indeed.

PHILOCRATES And so, I'm just telling you to remember: I am now not your master, but a slave. And I beg of you this one favour... Since the immortal gods have shown it their will that they want me, your master, to

33

be your fellow slave even though in times past I had the right to command you, I now pray of you... by uncertain Fortune, by the goodness my father showed you, by our common slavery at the hands of enemies...that you do not treat me with less honour than when you served me, and that you remember to remember who you were and who you are now.

TYNDARUS Yes, I'm you and you are me.

PHILOCRITUS Well, if you can remember that, there's hope in our deceit.

[2.2]

(*Enter* Hegio *from his house*)

HEGIO (*to those inside his house*) I'll be back when I have the information I want from these people.
(*to Overseer*) Where are those men I told you to bring to my door?

PHILOCRATES By the Gods, you've made sure you don't have far to look, given the number of chains and guards you've provided for us!

HEGIO The man who is wary of being deceived, is scarcely wary even when he's being wary. And even when he thought he was being wary, this particular cautious man has been caught out. And is it not entirely reasonable that I should keep close watch on you when I've paid so much for you – and in cash too!

PHILOCRATES We certainly can't criticize you if you keep a close eye on us: but neither can you criticize us if we take our opportunity and clear off.

HEGIO Just as you are prisoners here, so my son is a prisoner in your country.

PHILOCRATES He was captured?

HEGIO Yes.

PHILOCRATES So we're not alone in our feeble efforts.

HEGIO Come over here (*takes Philocrates to one side*)
There's some information I want from you
personally. And I don't want you to tell me any lies.

PHILOCRATES If I know the answer, I won't lie. And if
there's something I don't know, I'll still tell you what
I don't know.

TYNDARUS (*aside*) The old man is now at the barber's and
a shave awaits him! He (*indicating Philocrates*)
hasn't even put a towel round him to keep the hairs
off his clothes. Whether he's going to give him a
light trim or a close shave I've no idea, but if he's
careful, he'll give him a handsome haircut!

HEGIO (*to Philocrates*) Would you prefer to be a slave or a
free man; tell me.

PHILOCRATES I want to be as close to any up-sides and as
far from any down-sides as possible.
I must say, though, that slavery hasn't been so bad
for me: I wasn't treated any differently from the
master's son.

TYNDARUS (*aside*) Well done! I wouldn't swap him for a
Greek philosopher: they're not a patch on him!

HEGIO What family is Philocrates from (*indicating
Tyndarus*)?

PHILOCRATES His family name is …Megaplutocraticus:
the most powerful and honourable family in the area.

HEGIO What about him himself: is he respected?

PHILOCRATES Most respected! And by the top people!

HEGIO Is his family well off, would you say?

PHILOCRATES Well off?! They're rolling in it!

HEGIO What about his father? Is he still alive?

PHILOCRATES He was alive when we left. If you want to
know if he's alive now, you'll have to search the
Underworld.

TYNDARUS (*aside*) It's going well. He doesn't just lie, he
   speaks philosophy.

HEGIO What was his name?

PHILOCRATES He's called Midas Megaplutocraticus.

HEGIO His name derives from his riches no doubt?

PHILOCRATES (*slyly*) No, it's more to do with his greed
   and business acumen.

HEGIO What are you saying? ...that his father's tight-
   fisted?

PHILOCRATES I wouldn't just say he was tight-fisted: to
   give you an idea... When he sacrifices to his
   Guardian Spirit, in performing the rites, he uses the
   cheapest possible pottery in case the Spirit runs off
   with it! As you can see, he's not one to let anyone
   take advantage of him.

HEGIO So come back over here with me. (*They rejoin
   Tyndarus.*)
   (*aside*) I'm going to confirm the information I need
   from his master.
   (*to Tyndarus*) Philocrates, your man here has done
   what an honest man should do. I now know what
   family you're from: he has just told me. If you would
   like to confirm what he's said, you would be doing
   yourself a favour. However, I already have the
   information from him.

TYNDARUS He has done his duty by speaking the truth to
   you, although I would much have preferred to have
   kept my nobility, family and wealth well hidden,
   Hegio. However, now that I have lost my homeland
   and my freedom, I do not suppose it is reasonable to
   expect him to fear me rather than you.
   The forces of war have rendered my riches no greater
   than his. I remember when he used not to dare cross

me with a single word, but now he wounds me with impunity.

Do you not see? Fortune shapes and moulds our human lives, and has made me, once free, now a slave, once of the highest rank, now of the lowest, once used to giving orders, now serving the command of another.

However, if I now have a master similar to myself when I was in command of my household, I need not fear that his command will be unjust or burdensome.

I would like to say this to you, Hegio, unless you prefer me not to...

HEGIO Say what you will.

TYNDARUS I was once as free as your son; an enemy army took my freedom just as one took his; He is now a slave amongst our people just as I am now a slave amongst yours. There is undoubtedly a god who hears and sees our actions. He, in accordance with your treatment of me here, will care for him there. He will favour the deserving as he will be just towards the undeserving.

And as you long for your son, my father longs for me.

HEGIO I know. But do you agree with what he (*indicating Philocrates*) has told me?

TYNDARUS That my father has huge wealth at home, I admit, and also that I am born to the highest rank. But I beg you. Hegio, do not let my wealth sway your mind to be over-greedy. Even though I'm an only child, my father might think it more proper for me to be a slave in your house, well off at your expense and clothed by you, than for him to be reduced to beggary and consequent dishonour by your demands.

37

HEGIO I myself am not of the opinion that wealth is the be-
all and end-all in life. Indeed, I know that wealth has
made a fool of many a man, and is more often a
source of loss than gain. I hate gold! How often it has
given bad advice!

Now listen to what I have to say: I want you to know
my thoughts.

My son is a slave; he is held prisoner in your country,
Elis.

If you return him to me, you need not pay me a single
drachma in addition and I'll send you and him home.
You won't get home any other way.

TYNDARUS You are a fair man and you seek a fair
bargain. But is he a slave to some individual or to the
state?

HEGIO He is the slave of a private individual, a doctor
called Menarchus.

TYNDARUS (*aside*) By the gods, he's a client of his
(*indicating Philocrates*).

(*to Hegio*) This will be as easy as pie!

HEGIO Get him to ransom my son.

TYNDARUS I will. May I ask something of you, Hegio?

HEGIO Within reason.

TYNDARUS So then. I don't ask to be sent home myself
until your son returns. But I suggest that I am held
hostage here whilst he (*indicating Philocrates*)
returns to my father to secure the ransom of your son.

HEGIO No, no, I'd rather send someone else to meet your
father when there's a truce. He can take your
instructions and make sure they're carried out.

TYNDARUS There's no point sending someone he doesn't
know. You'll be wasting your time. Send him
(*indicating Philocrates*). He'll complete the whole
transaction if *he* goes there. You couldn't send

anyone more reliable ...nor whom my father would trust more ...nor a slave he would more approve of ...nor anyone to whom my father (I am prepared to say this boldly) would be more willing to entrust his own son. Have no concerns: it is at my risk that we put his loyalty to the test. I can rely on his character: he knows that I look after him.

HEGIO All right. I'll send him if you wish. You will act as surety for him.

TYNDARUS That's fine. I'd like this done as soon as possible.

HEGIO Have you any objection to paying me two thousand drachmas if he fails to return?

TYNDARUS No, that would be perfectly satisfactory.

(*Behind Hegio's back, Tyndarus looks surprised: where is he going to get 2,000 drachmas from if Philocrates fails to return?*)

HEGIO (*to Overseer*) Take this man's chains off ...and his as well!

(*Overseer takes the chains off both Tyndarus and Philocrates.*)

TYNDARUS (*to Hegio*) May all the Gods grant your every wish, for honouring me like this and releasing my chains! It's no unpleasant thing for my neck to be rid of that neck-band!

HEGIO One good turn deserves another: so if you're going to send him to your home, tell him fully and plainly what you want him to say to your father. Let's call him over.

TYNDARUS Please do.

[2.3]

HEGIO (*going to Philocrates*) May all turn out well for me, my son and for you two! I, your new master, want you to apply yourself loyally to doing what your old master tells you. Now, I'm handing you over to him on surety of two thousand drachmas. He says he's willing to send you to his father for him to secure the release of my son and then for him and me to arrange the exchange of our sons.

PHILOCRATES It's right I try to help both you and him. I'll be the go-between. And I'll go in either direction, as you instruct.

HEGIO You are greatly helping yourself in bearing your slavery as it should be born. Follow me.
(*Hegio and Philocrates rejoin Tyndarus.*)
(*to Tyndarus*) He's at your disposal.

TYNDARUS I thank you for giving me this opportunity to send him as a messenger to my parents. Once there, he will tell them, properly in order, what my circumstances here are and what action I would like my father to take.
(*to Philocrates*) This man and I, Tyndarus, have just now agreed that I am to send you to my father in Elis and I am to stand surety in the sum of two thousand drachmas against your failing to return.

PHILOCRATES That's a reasonable agreement. Your father will be waiting for me or some other messenger to come to him from here.

TYNDARUS So I want you to pay attention to the message I want you to take home to my father.

PHILOCRATES Philocrates, I will be as diligent as I have always been, and I will put body and soul into doing all I can to help you!

TYNDARUS That is as it should be. Now listen. First of all, give my regards to my mother and father and to my relatives and to anyone else you see who might have my interests at heart. Say that I am well and that I serve as a slave to this excellent gentleman who has treated me, and still does treat me, with considerable respect.

PHILOCRATES That's straightforward and easy enough to remember.

TYNDARUS Indeed, if it were not for my guard, I would consider myself a free man. But tell my father what agreement I have reached with this gentleman in respect of his son.

PHILOCRATES Pure and simply nothing simpler!

TYNDARUS Tell him to pay the doctor Menarchus a ransom for the son and then to send him here to be exchanged for the two of us.

PHILOCRATES I can remember that.

HEGIO Act as quickly as you can. Time is of the essence for both of us.

PHILOCRATES I can assure you: you will not wish to see your son any more than he will wish to see his.

HEGIO Indeed, each loves his own.

PHILOCRATES There's no further message, then?

TYNDARUS Er, well, say that I am well…

(suddenly seeing his opportunity) Ah yes, speak bravely, Tyndarus. Tell my father that there has never been any discord between us, that you have earned no reproach (and that I have not treated you unfairly) and that you have served your master as you ought in difficult circumstances; and that you have never failed me in thought or deed even as we teetered on the brink of destitution.

When my father hears, Tyndarus, of your loyalty to his son and to him himself, he will not be so greedy as not to set you free, free of charge. And if I return home, I will make every effort to make sure he does. After all, it is by your efforts, comradeship, courage and thoughtfulness that you have brought it about that I may be able to return to my parents again – by telling this gentleman of my wealthy family: indeed, your thoughtfulness in this respect has freed your master from his chains.

PHILOCRATES I have acted just as you have said, and I'm pleased you realise it. You deserve the way I've behaved towards you. In fact, Philocrates, if I were to recount all the many good things you've done for me, it would take me well into the night! Indeed, it has been as if you had been my slave: nothing less, you couldn't have been more compliant!

HEGIO By the Gods! What generosity of spirit these men have! They bring tears to my eyes! To see the love that exists between them! To see a slave praised and heap such praise upon his master!

TYNDARUS In fact, he doesn't heap on me one hundredth part of the praise that he himself deserves to be praised!

HEGIO And so, since you have both acted so well, now is the opportunity for you (*to Philocrates*) to crown your good deeds with a demonstration of faithfulness to him.

PHILOCRATES It is not merely a question of wanting: I shall make every effort to make this a success.

To be sure, Hegio, let Supreme Jupiter be my witness, I swear I shall not be unfaithful to Philocrates…!

HEGIO You're a fine man!

PHILOCRATES …and I would never have anything done to him that I wouldn't have done to myself!

TYNDARUS I want you to put these words to the test by your works and deeds. I have said less about you than I wanted: so pay attention. And do not be angry at my words. But, please, remember that you are being sent home with my acting as your surety: my life is pledged on your behalf. Don't you forget me the moment you are out of sight. You are leaving me here in slavery – for you – should you decide to consider yourself a free man and forfeit your security (*alluding to himself*), and make no effort to bring this man's son back. So, be faithful to the faithful and do not waver in your faithfulness!

Our father, I know, will do everything he should.

And so, keep me for ever as a friend and find this man (*Hegio*) a friend also whom we have found. I beg you, taking your right hand in mine, (*they clasp hands*) do not be less true to me than I am to you.

Go now! You now are my master, my patron, my father! To you I entrust my hopes and wellbeing.

PHILOCTRATES That's enough orders. Will you be satisfied if I return with mission accomplished?

TYNDARUS Certainly.

PHILOCRATES I shall return resplendent to satisfy both you (*indicating Hegio*) and you (*indicating Tyndarus*). Is there anything else?

TYNDARUS Get back as soon as you can.

PHILOCRATES I'll do my best.

HEGIO (*to Philocrates*) Follow me. I'll draw some money from my bankers for your journey and I'll obtain a letter of passage from the commanding officer.

TYNDARUS A letter of passage…?

HEGIO …which he can take to the army so that they'll let
him set off home.
(*to Tyndarus*) You now, go inside.
TYNDARUS Have a good journey.
PHILOCRATES Thank you; farewell.

(*Exeunt* Tyndarus *and* Overseer *into Hegio's house*)

HEGIO (*aside*) What a good idea it was to buy those two
prisoners from the officers! If the gods are willing, I
shall soon have my son out of his slavery. And to
think I hesitated so long over whether to buy them or
not!
(*to slaves indoors*) Slaves, watch that one indoors, if
you will. I don't want him setting a foot outside
without a guard.
(*aside*) I'll be making an appearance at home myself,
but I must go round to my brother's. I can check my
prisoners there and ask whether any of them knows
this young man (*indicating Philocrates*).
(*to Philocrates*) You, follow me. I want to get you on
your way. That's the first item on the agenda.

(*Exeunt* Hegio *and* Philocrates *along the street.*)

ACT 3

An hour or so later.

(*Enter* Ergasilus, *from along the street.*)

ERGASILUS   It's an unhappy man who looks for food and
   barely finds any; it's an even unhappier man who can
   barely look for food and finds none; but he is
   unhappiest of all who is absolutely starving and has
   nothing to eat. By Hercules, I could take Today and
   gouge its eyes out for imbuing every mortal man with
   a malignity towards me! Never have I seen a more
   barren day nor one so crammed full of famine: my
   stomach and gullet have sunk to a feast of fasting! A
   curse on the scrounger's art! – now that youth
   dissociates itself from the elegant poor. They have no
   time for us valiant warriors of no account, the butt of
   jokes, who have conversation but no food or money.
   No, they want companions who, when they are
   invited to dine, repay the compliment in their own
   homes. They even procure their own women – this
   used to be the prerogative of us scroungers – but now
   they leave the forum and go unashamedly to the slave
   dealers themselves – just as unashamedly as when
   they condemn those guilty defendants in court. They
   don't care half a drachma for the elegant
   conversationalist poor: they're all so in love with
   themselves!
   A little while ago, I left here and met up with some of
   the young men in the forum. "Hello" I said, "Where
   are we going to dinner?" They said nothing. "Come
   on; who's offering" I said. They were struck dumb.
   And they weren't joking. "Come on; where are we

45

dining?" I said. They just shook their heads. I told them a joke – one of my better ones that in the past would have secured me dinners for a month – but no one laughed. I soon saw this was planned. Even an irritated dog will show its teeth, but I couldn't get them show their teeth even with the tiniest smile. When I saw I was being made a fool of, I left them and went to talk to some others; then some others; and then some others. It was always the same. They were running a cartel – just like the oil merchants in the market at Velabrum[1]. So I've come back here, having been made a fool of there. In fact there were other scroungers walking about the forum to no avail. Now, by your (*indicating the Roman audience*) foreign law, I have a dead certain case: those who have plotted to deprive me of food and ruin my life, I'm going to sue: I'll win substantial damages: they can each provide me with ten dinners – on demand – when the price of food is high! That's what I'm going to do!

(*looking round, but seeing no one to sponge off*) Oh well, I'll go down to the port now: that's my one hope of finding dinner. And if that fails, then I'll come back here and cadge some ill-tasting food from the old man here.

(*Exit* Ergasilus, *along the street.*)

[1] Velabrum: a district of ancient Rome.

[3.2]
(*Enter* Hegio *and* Aristophontes *from Hegio's brother's house.*)

HEGIO (*aside*) What can be more pleasant than conducting business successfully and for the public good, just as I did yesterday, when I bought those prisoners? All who saw it, came up to me to congratulate me on my success! In fact, I felt exhausted by the time I had dealt with their hanging around me and their holding me back. I could scarcely extricate myself from their congratulations!
Eventually I made my way to the commanding officer; I asked for a letter of passage; it was provided immediately; I gave it to Tyndarus; he is now on his way home.
Then, when all was done, I immediately set off home, but went to my brother's where my other prisoners are. I asked them if anyone knew Philocrates from Elis. This man (*indicating Aristophontes*) shouted out that he was a close friend of his. I said he was at my house. He begged me to let him see him. I immediately ordered for his chains to be removed.
(*to Aristophontes*) Now you, follow me, so that the favour you ask can be granted and you can meet the man.

(*Exeunt* Hegio *and* Aristophontes *into Hegio's house.*)

[3.3]
(*Enter* Tyndarus, *rushing from Hegio's house*)

TYNDARUS (*aside*) At this moment, I would rather have lived than live! Now, all hope and resource is gone:

the auxiliaries have severed connections and left. This is the day when the possibility of keeping life and limb together has disappeared. No possible hope can dispel this fear of mine. Nowhere is a cloak to cover my clever subterfuge! I have no excuse for my lies nor hiding place for my trickery. My conspiracy cannot wait awhile at an inn, nor can my deceit put up at a lodging-house! What was covert is now overt! The illusion has been laid bare! Everything is in the open. There's nothing to discuss: I shall meet an early death – an untimely end on behalf of my master and myself! That Aristophontes, who has just gone into the house, has already destroyed me! He knew me; he's a close friend of Philocrates and a relation of his. Not even the Goddess of Wellbeing could now save me if she wanted to, and I'm going to have to think up an extremely clever plan by myself. But what, you poor fool? What contrivance can I devise? Actually, I'm clutching at straws. I'm in a mess!

[3.4]
(*Enter* Hegio, Aristophontes *and* Overseer *from Hegio's house*)

HEGIO That man who rushed out of the house – where on earth was he going?
TYNDARUS (*aside*) Now I'm really done for! The enemy approaches, Tyndarus! What shall I say? What story can I make up? What shall I deny? What shall I admit? It's all in the lap of the gods! I'll have to trust my own resources. I wish the gods had destroyed you, Aristophontes, long before you left home and came here to render my successful plan unsuccessful.

It's in ruins unless I can find some completely invincible solution.

HEGIO (*to Aristophontes, pointing to Tyndarus*) There he is! Go and speak to him!

TYNDARUS (*aside*) What man is in a worse state than I?

ARISTOPHONTES Why is it that I must say that you seem to be avoiding my gaze, Tyndarus, and to be treating me as a stranger – as if you didn't know me? I'm now a slave just as much as you, even though at home I was free whilst, from your childhood, you were a slave in Elis.

HEGIO I must say, I'm not surprised he's avoiding your gaze and finds you offensive when you call him 'Tyndarus' instead of 'Philocrates'!

TYNDARUS Hegio, this man was considered a raving lunatic in Elis and you mustn't let your ears be filled with his tales! At home he attacked his mother and father with a spear and he suffers from rabid fits! So, I'd keep well out of his way!

HEGIO (*to Overseer*) Well, get him out of my way!

(*Overseer restrains Aristophontes*)

ARISTOPHONTES What did you say, you liar! I'm a raving lunatic who chased my father with a spear and I suffer from rabid fits?!

HEGIO Don't worry: people get over rabid fits.

ARISTOPHONTES What! Do you believe him?!

HEGIO Believe what?

ARISTOPHONTES That I'm insane.

TYNDARUS (*to Hegio*) Look at his face – see how he stares at you! You'd better go! It's happening as I said – his rabies is flaring up! Take care!

HEGIO I knew he was mad the moment he called you 'Tyndarus'.

49

TYNDARUS Yes, and sometimes he even forgets his own name and doesn't know who he is!

HEGIO He even said he was a close friend of yours...

TYNDARUS (*sarcastically*) ...yes, and I suppose other famous madmen – Alcmaeon, Orestes and Lycurgus – are all close friends of mine!

ARISTOPHONTES (*to Tyndarus*) You slave! You dare to speak like that about me?! You say I don't know who you are?!

HEGIO Come now; it's obvious you don't know him: you call him 'Tyndarus' not 'Philocrates'. The man you can see, you plainly don't know. And you call him the name of a man you can't see!

ARISTOPHONTES On the contrary: he says he is a man he is not, and denies he is the man he is!

TYNDARUS (*throughout, trying to get Aristophontes to perceive there is a ruse and to go along with it*) So, you're the person to show that *Philocrates is not Philocrates*?

ARISTOPHONTES Well now, as I see it, you're the person to show that black is not black but white! Right, by Hercules – look me in the eye!

TYNDARUS (*looking Aristophontes in the eye*) Hmm?

ARISTOPHONES So then, tell me, do you deny that you are Tyndarus?

TYNDARUS I do deny it.

ARISTOPHONTES And you are saying that you are Philocrates?

TYNDARUS Yes, that's what I am *saying*.

ARISTOPHONTES (*to Hegio*) And you believe him?

HEGIO More than you – or indeed myself. You see, the man you say he is, set off today for Elis – to his father.

ARISTOPHONTES What father?! He's a slave!

TYNDARUS Look, you are a slave, but once you were free, as I trust I shall be myself, if only I can restore the son of this man (*indicating Hegio*) to his freedom.

ARISTOPHONTES What's that, you slave? Are you suggesting you were born a free man?

TYNDARUS I am suggesting you call me not *Freeman,* but *Philocrates.*

ARISTOPHONTES What's that? This is nonsense, Hegio: he's having you on. He's a slave himself, and he never owned a slave himself – apart from himself perhaps!

TYNDARUS Just because you yourself lived in poverty in your homeland, you want everyone to appear similar to yourself. That's not surprising: it's typical of the badly-off to hate and begrudge the well-off.

ARISTOPHONTES Hegio, please make sure you're not so rash as to continue to believe this man. And, I see, he has already given battle, so to speak: but in saying he is going to recover your son, he doesn't please me at all.

TYNDARUS I know you don't want this to happen. However, I will achieve it, if the gods are willing. I will restore him to this man. He, on the other hand, will restore me to my father in Elis. Hence, *I sent Tyndarus* to his father.

ARISTOPHONTES But you are he! And there's no other slave of that name in Elis except you.

TYNDARUS Are you going to carry on accusing me of being a slave – something that in fact arose through enemy action?

ARISTOPHONTES I can't contain myself any longer!

TYNDARUS (*to Hegio*) What?! Did you hear that? You'd better leave quickly! He'll start throwing stones at us if you don't have him seized!

ARISTOPHONTES This is all too much!

TYNDARUS His eyes are ablaze! He's having a fit! See how his whole body is dappled with lurid marks! Black bile is making him shake!

ARISTOPHONTES By the Gods, if this old man (*indicating Hegio*) knew what was going on, it would be an executioner's black burning pitch that would be making you shake and would be lighting up your head!

TYNDARUS He's delirious! Demons have him! By Hercules, (*to Hegio*) you'd do well to order him to be seized!

ARISTOPHONTES This is torture! If only I had a stone to knock his brains out. That would stop his torment! His words are ringing in my mind and driving me mad!

TYNDARUS Did you hear that?! He's looking for a stone!

ARISTOPHONTES Hegio, can I have a word with you, one to one?

HEGIO If you've something to say, say it where you are. I can hear you.

TYNDARUS By the Gods, don't go any nearer: he'll take your nose off with one bite!

ARISTOPHONTES (*to Hegio*) Ridiculous! You must not believe I'm insane, Hegio, or ever have been! Nor that I am ill as he says. But if you're afraid, order for me to be bound. I'm happy to be, provided that he is bound as well.

TYNDARUS No, no, Hegio. Just let him be bound if he wants it.

ARISTOPHONTES (*to Tyndarus*) You be quiet. I will ensure that you, you false Philocrates, are shown today to be the real Tyndarus.

(Behind Hegio's back, Tyndarus shakes his head frantically at Aristophontes)

(to Tyndarus) Why are you shaking your head at me?

TYNDARUS Me? …shake my head at you?

ARISTOPHONTES *(to Hegio)* What would he not do if you weren't here?

HEGIO What am I to make of all this?

What if I were to go up to this madman?

TYNDARUS Dear me, he'll make a fool of you! He's talking gibberish: you'll not make head nor tail of it! If he wore the right costume, you could take him for that other madman, Ajax!

HEGIO Possibly; but I'll go up to him anyway.

TYNDARUS *(aside)* I'm done for now! I'm on the altar with the knife at my throat! What can I do?!

HEGIO I'm listening, Aristophontes, in case you have something important to say?

ARISTOPHONTES You will hear the truth form me, Hegio, even though you now think it false. Firstly, I want to vindicate myself in your eyes: that I am not insane nor have any ailment – except being a slave. And so, may the King of the Gods and men restore me to my homeland: that man there is no more Philocrates than you or I.

HEGIO So tell me: who is he then?

ARISTOPHONTES He's the man I said he was at the start. And if you find otherwise, I shall plead no defence to my losing my parents and freedom in your house.

HEGIO *(to Tyndarus)* And what do you say?

TYNDARUS …that I am your slave and you my master.

HEGIO That's not what I asked you. Did you used to be a free man?

TYNDARUS I did.

ARISTOPHONTES He wasn't. He's talking nonsense!

TYNDARUS   What do you know about it? Were you perhaps my mother's midwife – to be able to speak with such presumption?

ARISTOPHONTES   As a boy, I used to see you: you were a boy also.

TYNDARUS   Well, as an adult I can see you: you are an adult also. So what? I wouldn't concern yourself with my affairs, if I were you. I don't concern myself with yours, do I?

HEGIO   (*to Aristophontes*) Was this man's father called Megaplutocraticus?

ARISTOPHONTES   No, I've never heard that name before. Philocrates' father was Theodoromedes.

TYNDARUS   (*aside*) I'm done for! Can you not be quiet, my heart? Go and be crucified! You beat and thump: I, poor wretch, can scarcely stand up for fear!

HEGIO   (*to Aristophontes*) Am I to believe, then, that this man was a slave in Elis and is definitely not Philocrates?

ARISTOPHONTES   Absolutely; without a shadow of doubt. But where is Philocrates?

HEGIO   He is where he most wants to be and where I don't want him to be. But still, is there any doubt…?

ARISTOPHONTES   …there's no doubt. I'm absolutely sure.

HEGIO   Sure?

ARISOPHONTES   Certainly. You'll never find anything more sure! Philocrates has been a friend of mine ever since we were boys.

HEGIO   Then I've been cruelly fleeced and dismembered by the tricks of this evil man (*indicating Tyndarus*), who has had me torn apart at his will by his deceit!
But what does your comrade Philocrates look like?

ARISTOPHONTES   I'll tell you: he has a thin face, a pointed nose, pale complexion, and reddish curly hair.

HEGIO It is becoming clear…

TYNDARUS (*aside*) …that I am heading, by Hercules, for complete and utter destruction! I even feel sorry for the whips that are about to die on my back!

HEGIO …that I have been tricked.

TYNDARUS Chains and fetters: what is stopping you coming to grip my limbs so that I can look after you?!

HEGIO Yes, those cheating slaves have certainly taken me in. The one who's gone pretended to be the slave whilst this one pretended to be the master. I've let go the kernel and kept its shell as security. I've been so stupid: they've really pulled the wool over my eyes! (*indicating Tyndarus*) But *he*'s not going to laugh at me much longer! (*calling to those in the house*) By the Gods, you inside, bring your whips out here!

[3.5]

(*Enter* Colax *and other* Servants, *bearing whips*)

COLAX Do you want us to fetch some timber to string him up on?

HEGIO Bind his hands tightly! (*Overseer complies*)

TYNDARUS What's all this?! What have I done wrong?

HEGIO You ask me that: you who sow crimes, plough the land for crimes, yes, and reap your criminal rewards!

TYNDARUS You've forgotten to mention the harrow. Farmers always use a harrow as well, you know.

HEGIO You seem confident as you stand before me.

TYNDARUS It is right that an innocent slave, one that has done no wrong, should be confident, especially before his own master.

HEGIO (*to Overseer*) Make sure his hands are fastened tight! (*The Overseer applies additional bonds*)

TYNDARUS (*presenting his hands*) I am yours and you can order these to be cut off if you like! But what is all this? What is it that makes you so angry with me?

HEGIO You have shattered and crushed me and everything dear to me by your falsehoods and deceits. My hopes rested in you alone, but you have destroyed the plans and opportunity that I had. You deprived me of Philocrates through your lies: I believed him to be the slave and you the master, just as you said. However, you had swapped names.

TYNDARUS I admit it. Everything is as you say. Thanks to a lie, he is away from you – thanks also to my efforts and quick-wittedness.

But, by Hercules, do you really hold that against me?!

HEGIO Clearly, since I am about to have you tortured to death!

TYNDARUS I am unconcerned if I die, having done nothing wrong.

If I do die here, and if he does not come back as he promised to, then by my death I will have achieved something memorable: I shall have freed my master, who was held captive, from slavery at the hands of his enemies, and shall have restored him, as a free man, to his father and to his homeland; and I shall have chosen rather to put my life at risk than that he should perish!

HEGIO You'll find your glory washes off in the rivers of the Underworld!

TYNDARUS A man acting through virtue may perish, but he does not die.

HEGIO When I have tortured and killed you for your trickery, they can choose whether they announce that you have died or perished. It does not matter which, so long as you are dead! Indeed, they can say you're alive if they want to!

TYNDARUS By Castor, if you do as you say, you'll face the consequences if my master comes back – which I'm sure he will!

ARISTOPHONTES (*suddenly realizing he's put his foot in it*) Oh! I get it now! By the Immortal Gods! Now I understand what's happened. My friend Philocrates has gained his freedom: he's back home with his father. That's good, and there's no one I'd be more pleased for. But I feel pretty sick that I've caused him (*indicating Tyndarus*) so much trouble. He's all tied up now thanks to me and my big mouth!

HEGIO (*to Tyndarus*) Did I not today forbid you to tell me anything that was untrue?

TYNDARUS You did.

HEGIO So, why did you dare to lie to me?

TYNDARUS Because the truth stood in the way of him whom I wished to help. Falsity, however stood to help him.

HEGIO Well, it will now stand in your way.

TYNDARUS It's for the best. I have saved my master, and I rejoice that he is saved – particularly as his father provided him with me to watch over him.

But do you think I acted wrongly?

HEGIO Completely!

TYNDARUS I think differently to you; I say I acted correctly. Now think, if someone had acted in that way towards your son, how thankful you would have been. You would grant such a slave his freedom, wouldn't you? You'd regard it much to his credit, wouldn't you?

(*Hegio hestitates*)

Wouldn't you?

HEGIO Perhaps so.

TYNDARUS Then why are you angry with *me*?

HEGIO Because you were more faithful to him than to me.

TYNDARUS What?! I'm a new, recently captured slave, owned by you for a night and a day, and you expect to instruct me to serve your interests in preference to those of him with whom I have spent my life since boyhood?

HEGIO Then expect your thanks from him!

(*to Overseer*) Take him and put him in thick heavy chains!

(*to Tyndarus*) Then, you will go to the stone-quarries, and whilst the rest of them dig out eight blocks of stone each, unless you do a day and a half's work each day, your name will become 'Six-hundred-lashes'!

ARISTOPHONTES By all Gods and men, I beg you, Hegio, don't have him destroyed in this way!

HEGIO He'll be taken good care of! At night he'll be bound and kept under guard. By day, he'll quarry stone underground. His torture will be continuous: there'll not be a single day's respite.

ARISTOPHONTES Are you resolved on this?

HEGIO Nothing is more certain than death!

(*to Overseer*) Take him straight to Hippolytus the blacksmith. Tell him to weld heavy chains on him. Then take him outside the city to my freedman Cordalus and make sure he takes him to the quarries.

Tell him to take such good care of him that nothing worse happens to him than the absolute worst!

TYNDARUS   What's the point of asking to be treated properly when clearly you are unwilling? The risk to my life is at your risk also.

After death, there is nothing to fear about death. And even if I survive a full lifetime, it will be but a short space of time in which to endure what is threatened.

(*to Hegio*) Farewell and may the Gods be with you – although you do not merit my good wishes.

(*to Aristophontes*) As for you, Aristophontes, may you 'fare' as 'well' as you deserve by me, since I'm in this state because of you.

HEGIO   Take him away.

TYNDARUS   There is one thing I ask. If Philocrates returns, I would like you to give me the opportunity to meet him.

HEGIO   (*to Overseer*) You'll be dead as well if you don't take him (*seizing hold of Tyndarus in a threatening manner*) out of my sight this instant!

(*The Overseer also seizes hold of Tyndarus, attempting to pull him away from Hegio*)

TYNDARUS   This is a use of force, by Hercules: I'm being pushed and pulled at the same time!

(*Exeunt* Overseer *and* Tyndarus, *Overseer leading Tyndarus away along the street.*
Exeunt Colax *and* Servants *into Hegio's house*)

HEGIO   (*aside*) He's off straight to his prison cell as he deserves.

It'll be a lesson to all my other captives not to dare to commit crimes against me. If it hadn't been for this man here (*indicating Aristophontes*), who brought everything to light, they really would have taken me for a ride. In the future, I'll trust no one in anything. I can be taken in once, but that's enough.

Yes, I was fool enough to think I could buy my son back out of slavery. That hope has gone. I lost one son, a four-year-old whom a slave stole from me; and I've found no trace of my boy or the slave since. And my elder boy is in the hands of our enemies. Why have the gods taken such offence? Have I produced children in order to be childless?

(*to Aristophontes*) Follow me. I'm taking you back where you came from.

(*aside*) I feel sorry for no one, since no one feels sorry for me.

ARISTOPHONTES I drew omen from out of those chains. I'll have to put that omen, and myself, back into those chains.

(*Exeunt* Aristophontes *and* Hegio *into Hegio's brother's house.*)

ACT 4

Several weeks have passed [1].

(*Enter* Egasilus *from along the street*)

ERGASILUS   Supreme Jupiter, you are my saviour and benefactor! You offer me sumptuous abundance and praise, profit, sport, fun, festivity, feasting, a procession of dinners, a glut of drink and joy, and never will I have to beg anyone for anything ever again!
Now I can help a friend or destroy an enemy – to such an extent has this day bestowed on me delightfully its delightful delightfulness! I have received a fat legacy with no strings attached!
I am now making my way to old man Hegio, to whom I am bringing exactly what he has prayed to the gods for, and more. The matter is settled – just as slaves in comedies usually settle matters. I shall now wrap my cloak around my neck, so that I can run and make sure I am the first to tell him. And I hope that my message supplies me with never-ending food!

---

[1] Ie. several weeks have passed in the lives of all the characters in the play except Ergasilus, who speaks as if returning from the port to which he ventured in search of dinner earlier in the day in Act 3.1.

[4.2]
(*Enter* Hegio *from his house*)

HEGIO   (*aside*) The more I mull this matter over in my
mind, the more I feel quite sick! I've been taken to
the cleaners, and I didn't see it coming! When all this
gets out, I'll be a laughing-stock! When I appear in
the forum, they'll all say to each other "Here's that
learned gentleman who's been made a fool of".
But is that Ergasilus I see over there? Why is his
cloak wrapped around his neck? What's he doing
here?

ERGASILUS   (*aside, in mock self-important manner*) Cast
off delay, Ergasilus, and proceed! I give due warning
that no man should stand in my way unless he feels
he has lived long enough! He who gets in my way
will suffer the consequences! (*He squares up like a
boxer taking guard*)

HEGIO   Has he taken up boxing?

ERGASILUS   Right then! Let everyone mind their *own*
business and certainly not bring it into this street! My
fist is my siege-weapon, my forearm my catapult, my
upper arm my battering-ram, and I can down anyone
with my knee; anyone I take on will pick their teeth
up later...!

HEGIO   (*aside*) Why so threatening? I cannot imagine.

ERGASILUS   ...Yes, he'll remember the time and place!

HEGIO   I wonder what the cause of all this is.

ERGASILUS   I give prior notice, (don't say you were not
warned) confine yourselves to your homes; do not
resist my force!

HEGIO   All I can say is, to have such confidence, he must
have managed to fill his stomach. And I pity the poor
man by whose food this imperiousness arose!

ERGASILUS And as for those pig-breeding millers who feed stuffing to their pigs whose stench prevents anyone from walking past the mills, if I see one of their sows wandering about, I'll knock the stuffing out of its master with these fists!

HEGIO Regal, indeed, imperial edicts! Yes, he must have a full stomach.

ERGASILUS And as for those fish-mongers who sell rotten fish as they ride around on their clip-clopping geldings, and whose smell drives all the shoppers into the forum, I'll beat them up with their own fish-baskets, so that they know what annoyance they cause to other people's noses!

And as for those butchers, who shout about the sheep they've deprived of their lambs, and who offer lambs for slaughter but have only slaughtered lamb at twice the price, and who describe some aged ram as the bellwether of their flock, if I see one of those butchers and his old ram on the public highway, I'll render both butcher and ram into mincemeat!

HEGIO Well now, he's issuing orders like a magistrate. I'm surprised the Aetolians haven't put him in charge of food standards!

ERGASILUS I'm now no scrounger but a king more kingly than kingliness, now that so many provisions are in the port destined for my stomach, – yes, food!

But I delay in my mission to bring happiness to old man Hegio: is there any man alive equally fortunate as he?

HEGIO What is this happiness that this happy man is about to heap upon me?

ERGASILUS (*knocking loudly on the door of Hegio's house*) Hey! Where are you? Is anyone in? Will someone open this door?

HEGIO This man is inviting himself to dinner at my house!

ERGASILUS (*loudly*) If someone doesn't open this door soon, I'll kick it down!

HEGIO Perhaps I ought to speak to the man.
(*from across the street*) Ergasilus!

ERGASILUS Who's calling out my name?

HEGIO Over here! Look!

ERGASILUS (*disdainfully, without looking*) Good Fortune never looks over there: so why should I. Who is it, anyway?

HEGIO It's me, Hegio.

ERGASILUS (*approaching Hegio*) Ah! Most excellent of excellent personages, you are here at exactly the right time!

HEGIO You've met someone or other at the port to dine with: that's why you were being so disdainful.

ERGASILUS Give me your hand (*proffering his own*).

HEGIO (*unimpressed*) My hand?

ERGASILUS Give me your hand this instant!

HEGIO Here. (*Then Ergasilus enthusiastically shakes Hegio's hand*)

ERGASILUS Rejoice!

HEGIO At what am I to rejoice?

ERGASILUS Because I tell you to. Come on, rejoice!

HEGIO I'm afraid my grief supersedes any rejoicing.

ERGASILUS But I shall erase any stains of grief that haunt you! Be bold! Rejoice!

HEGIO So I rejoice, but I still don't know what I'm rejoicing at.

ERGASILUS Good, Now give the order…

HEGIO Order? Order for what?

ERGASILUS …for a great fire to be lit!

HEGIO A great fire to be lit?

ERGASILUS That's right. Make sure it's a big one!

HEGIO What?! You idiot, do you think I'm going to burn my house down for your sake?!

ERGASILUS Don't be angry.
Well, aren't you going to order the cooking pots to be set out, the pans to be washed, the bacon and the banquet to be baked and boiled, bubbling hot for our bowls? Is anyone going to go and buy some fish...?

HEGIO (*aside*) The man's a dreamer!

ERGASILUS ...and some pork and lamb and chicken...?

HEGIO You know how to live well; if only you could pay for it!

ERGASILUS ...and some gammon and lamprey and pickled mackerel and stingray and dog-fish and soft cheese?

HEGIO At my house, Ergasilus, you can name all these things, but don't expect to eat them.

ERGASILUS Do you think I'm suggesting all this for me?

HEGIO Be under no illusion; here you will eat either nothing, or not much more. So if you are here with an appetite, it must be for plain food.

ERGASILUS And so I would, but you will want something grander, even if *I* were to say no.

HEGIO I would?

ERGASILUS Yes, you would.

HEGIO If you say so.

ERGASILUS I'm ready to help. Do you want me to make you a man blessed with good fortune?

HEGIO Well, rather than one who is not.

ERGASILUS Give me your hand! (*proffering his own*)

HEGIO My hand?

ERGASILUS The gods favour you!

HEGIO I think not.

ERGASILUS You are amongst the thorns and see only thorny problems. But order for purified vessels be

65

brought for religious ceremony and have a fat lamb made ready.

HEGIO Why?

ERGASILUS For sacrifice.

HEGIO To which god?

ERGASILUS But, by Hercules, *I* am you great Jupiter, and I am also your gods of Wellbeing, Good Fortune, Light, Joy and Rejoicing. And you should propitiate these gods with plenty of food!

HEGIO I feel you are hungry.

ERGASILUS No, *I* feel I am hungry.

HEGIO As you will: I can easily accommodate your little joke...

ERGASILUS ...as the High Priest said to the actor!

HEGIO (*unamused*) May Jupiter and all the gods destroy you...!

ERGASILUS ...destroy you, by Hercules! I should be thanked for my news – the good news I now report from the port! You will be pleased!

HEGIO Clear off, you idiot! You're too late to bring me any good news!

ERGASILUS If I'd come earlier, you might have said that. But now, accept the joy I bring!

Your son, Philopolemus, I have just seen, in the port, alive, safe and sound, just off a ship, and with him, that young Elean prisoner, and also that slave of yours, Stalagmus, who fled your house, stealing your little four-year-old son!

HEGIO Don't be ridiculous!

ERGASILUS The holy Goddess of Satedness will love me, Hegio, and may she bless me with her name for ever, as I did see ....

HEGIO ...My son?

ERGASILUS ...your son and my guardian spirit!

HEGIO   And you saw that Elean whom I had held
     captive...?
ERGASILUS Yes, by Apollo!
HEGIO ... and that slave of mine, Stalagmus, who stole my
     son?
ERGASILUS Yes, by the city of Cora!
HEGIO Am I now to believe it?
ERGASILUS Yes, by the city of Praeneste!
HEGIO He's here?
ERGASILUS Yes, by the city of Signia!
HEGIO You're certain?
ERGASILUS Yes, by the city of Frusino!
HEGIO Now please...
ERGASILUS Yes, by the city of Alatrium!
HEGIO Why do you keep swearing by Italian cities?
ERGASILUS   Because they're as unappealing as you say
     your meals are!
HEGIO You're talking nonsense!
ERGASILUS I'm speaking the truth: it's just that you're not
     believing me.
     Now, your slave Stalagmus, escaped from you didn't
     he, and thought he was free?
HEGIO Yes he did.
ERGASILUS Well, he wasn't free when we found him: A
     woman from Northern Italy had collared him and
     clearly had him in under her thumb!
HEGIO Are you really telling me this in good faith?
ERGASILUS Yes indeed.
HEGIO By the Immortal Gods, I feel reborn, if what you're
     saying is true!
ERGASILUS   What's that? You still have doubts, even
     though I swear solemnly it's true?
     Hegio, if my solemn oath counts for so little, go
     down to the port and see for yourself.

HEGIO I will. You go inside and make the necessary preparations. Use what you want, place any orders, empty our storerooms. I appoint you my steward.

ERGASILUS And, by Hercules, if I prove a false prophet about your son, you can thrash me to pieces!

HEGIO I shall provide you with feasts for ever, if you're telling the truth.

ERGASILUS Paid for by…?

HEGIO …by me and my son.

ERGASILUS Do you swear to this?

HEGIO I swear to it.

ERGASILUS In return, I say your son has arrived.

HEGIO Make the best preparations you can!

(*Exit* Hegio *along the street*)

[4.3]

ERGASILUS (*calling after Hegio*) Have a good walk there – and back.

(*aside*) He's gone. And he's entrusted the top job – concerning food – to me.

By the Immortal Gods, let's cut up some carcasses; let's hammer the hams, get the bacon bubbling, titivate the tripe, and get the fat frying! Those butchers and pork dealers are going to earn their keep! But let's not waste time *talking* about culinary matters: I shall now go, in accordance with my official position, to pronounce judgment on the bacon and to render help to any hams that are in suspense untried.

(*Exit* Ergasilus *into Hegio's house*)

[4.4]
(Alarmed slaves can be heard from inside Hegio's house.
Enter Boy, *in distress, from Hegio's house)*

BOY   May Jupiter and the Gods destroy you, Ergasilus, and that stomach of yours, and all scroungers, and all who give scroungers their dinner!
A disastrous raging storm has made its way into our house! He's like a ravenous wolf – I thought he was going to attack me! When I saw his hungry face, I began to fear for my life; it was the way he gnashed his teeth! He came like a whirlwind round the meat and meat hooks! He seized a sword and cut off chunks of meat from three carcasses; he smashed all the jars and pots that were less than half-full; and he told the cook to boil up the jars for preserves! He broke into every room and opened up all the cupboards!
(to those indoors) Watch him, will you! I'm off to meet the old man. I'll say he needs to buy some more food, if he wants to eat any himself! The way that man's going about it *(indicating Hegio's house)*, there's either nothing left or there soon won't be!

(Exit Boy *along the street)*

ACT 5

(*Enter* Hegio, Philopolemus, Philocrates, *and* Stalagmus, *the last in chains*)

HEGIO (*to Philopolemus*) I give Jupiter and all the Gods heartfelt thanks for bringing you back to your father and for relieving me of all the worry which I had to endure whilst I was deprived of you; and also for being able to see this man (*indicating Stalagmus*) in our power, and for benefiting from the good faith shown by this man (*indicating Philocrates*) towards us.

PHILOPOLEMUS Enough of the suffering I've endured and enough of the many tears I've shed; enough also of the distress you have suffered which you told me about at the port! There's a more important matter.

PHILOCRATES What other matter is there? I kept faith with you and secured your son his freedom.

HEGIO You have acted, Philocrates, in such a way that I could never thank you enough for the service you have rendered me and my son.

PHILOPOLEMUS But you can, father. You will be able, and I will be able, and the gods will give us the power to do a deserved favour to one who has earned such kindness. And so, father, you *can* act towards this man (*indicating Philocrates*) as he deserves.

HEGIO What more can I say? There is no possible way in which I can deny what you ask.

PHILOCRATES I ask of you that you return me that slave that I left here as surety for me and who has always been truer to me than to himself, so that I can reward him for his good services to me.

HEGIO For your service to me, I am pleased to grant your request and, indeed, any other request you might have. And I hope you're not annoyed that, in anger, I treated him badly.

PHILOCRATES Why, what did you do?

HEGIO I had him put in chains and set to work in the quarries, when I realised I'd been tricked.

PHILOCRATES Oh no! To think how this finest of men suffered on account of me!

HEGIO Well, because of this, don't pay me a single drachma for him. Take him free of charge – and set him free.

PHILOCRATES Well now, Hegio, that's kind of you. So please, have the man brought here.

HEGIO Certainly.

(*calling inside his house to the Overseer*) Where are you?! Go immediately and fetch Tyndarus here!

(*to Philopolemus and Philocrates*) You two go inside and bathe after your journey.

In the meantime, I'm going to ask this good-for-nothing slave (*indicating Stalagmus*) what became of my younger son!

PHILOPOLEMUS This way, Philocrates.

PHILOCRATES Thank you.

(*Exeunt* Philopolemus *and* Philocrates *into Hegio's house*)

[5.2]

HEGIO Now then, my fine fellow, whom I actually paid good money for!

STALAGMUS What must I do when such a man as you is ready to affirm what is false? I have been a man of elegance and wit – a good man, never; an honest man, never. I won't be changing my ways. Don't make the mistake of thinking I will ever be honest.

HEGIO   You understand pretty well where your fortunes stand at present. If you are truthful, for your part, you'll be making a bad state of affairs slightly better. Speak rightly and truly, even though you've never done anything right or true before.

STALAGMUS   Do you think I'll be ashamed of what I say just because you say I should?

HEGIO   I'll make you ashamed and red in the face: in fact, you'll be a mass of red when I've finished with you!

STALAGMUS   I do believe I'm being threatened with a whipping! How unusual! So do it! Say what you're doing, then do what you want!

HEGIO   Enough of your eloquence! Keep it for later!

STALAGMUS   Please yourself.

HEGIO   (*aside*) And he was so obedient as a boy.
(*to Stalagmus*) But down to business. Now pay attention and answer my questions!

STALAGMUS   This is nonsense! Don't you think I know what I deserve?

HEGIO   Well, you have a chance of escaping some of it, if not all.

STALAGMUS   I'm sure I won't escape much. There's much in store for me, and it's my fault, since I ran away, stole your son and sold him!

HEGIO   Who to?

STALAGMUS   To a man in Elis called Theodoromedes for six hundred drachmas.

HEGIO   But, by the Immortal Gods, that's the father of Philocrates here!

STALAGMUS   Well, I know him better than you: and I've seen him more often.

HEGIO Supreme Jupiter save me and my son! (*calling inside his house*) Philocrates, by your guardian spirt, I beg you come out here!

[5.3]
(*Enter* Philocrates *from Hegio's house*)

PHILOCRATES Hegio, here I am. Please tell me what you want.
HEGIO This man says he sold my son in Elis for six hundred drachmas to your father.

(*Philocrates leads Stalagmus away from Hegio, so that Hegio does not fully hear the questions and answers*)

PHILOCRATES How long ago was this?
STALAGMUS About twenty years ago.
PHILOCRATES (*to the distant Hegio*) His memory is false.
STALAGMUS Either mine or yours. Your father, when you were a small boy yourself, gave you a four-year-old boy to have as your own.
PHILOCRATES What was his name? Speak the truth and tell me.
STALAGMUS To begin with you called him 'Paegnium', but later you gave him the name 'Tyndarus'.
PHILOCRATES How come I don't know you?
STALAGMUS It is usual for people to forget or simply not to know those who can be of no benefit to them.
PHILOCRATES Tell me, was the boy you sold my father the same as the one who was given to me?
STALAGMUS Yes, (*indicating Hegio*) he was his son.
HEGIO (*joining the pair; to Stalagmus*) Is he alive – this man?

73

STALAGMUS I took the money: I didn't care about the rest.

HEGIO (*to Philocrates*) What do you think?

PHILOCRATES That this man Tyndarus is your son! That's what he (*indicating Stalagmus*) says, anyway. And Tyndarus as a boy was brought up well and properly with me as a boy – right through to adulthood.

HEGIO Then I feel both bad and fortunate, if what you both say is true.

I feel bad about the way I have treated him if he is my own son. Oh dear! How much more, and in other ways, how much less I've done than I ought! I am now racked with guilt at my ill treatment of him! If only I could undo what I've done!

But see; here he comes – in chains!

[5.4]

(*Enter* Tyndarus, *exhausted, in chains and carrying a crowbar, and* Overseer)

TYNDARUS (*aside*) I have often seen depictions of the tortures of the Underworld, but no tortures rival those that I have experienced in the quarries. For there is the place where any thoughts of tiredness are driven from the body by hard labour. Well-off children are given pet birds to play with: well, as soon as I arrived in the quarry, I was given this pet crow (*indicating his crowbar*) as my constant companion.

Well, there's my master in the doorway.

And there also is my other master returned from Elis!

HEGIO Ah, my long-lost son!

TYNDARUS Son? Oh, is that a joke... that like a parent he's just brought me into the light of day?

PHILOCRATES Good day, Tyndarus!

TYNDARUS You as well? It was for your sake I'm in this mess!

PHILOCRATES In fact, I'm just bringing you into freedom and wealth!

This (*indicating Hegio*) is your father!

And this (*indicating Stalagmus*) is the slave who stole you from him when you were a four-year-old. He sold you to my father for six hundred drachmas, and he gave you as a boy to me as a boy to be my own. He has given us proof of all this – we've just brought him back from Elis.

TYNDARUS Haven't you brought a son back from Elis?

PHILOCRATES Yes! And you'll soon see your own brother inside (*indicating Hegio's house*)!

TYNDARUS By Hercules! I do have a vague memory that my father was called Hegio.

HEGIO I am he!

PHILOCRATES I suggest that your son become lighter by the weight of those chains and that your slave become heavier by the same amount!

HEGIO (*to Tyndarus*) Yes, we must have that seen to. Let's go indoors and have a blacksmith come to relieve you of your chains. We can give them to him (*indicating Stalagmus*).

STALAGMUS How generous: I certainly don't have anything else to call mine.

EPILOGUE spoken by a member of the cast

Audience! Our play has been presented as a respectable drama. In it there have been no illicit love affairs, no swapping of babies, no defrauding of money, nor has a young man in love set a slave girl free without his father's knowledge.
Playwrights write few plays of this sort, in which good men are made better.
So please, if you have enjoyed our play and we have not disappointed you, signal your approval!
Reward our respectability and give us your applause!

www.ingramcontent.com/pod-product-compliance
Lightning Source LLC
Chambersburg PA
CBHW070313290526
45791CB00003B/1108